50 Poland Restaurant Bread Recipes for Home

By: Kelly Johnson

Table of Contents

- Chleb Wiejski
- Chleb Żytni
- Chleb Pszenno-Żytni
- Chleb Rzemieślniczy
- Chleb Tattarski
- Chleb Grahamski
- Chleb Słodowy
- Chleb Na Zakwasie
- Chleb Kukurydziany
- Chleb Miejski
- Chleb Ziemniaczany
- Chleb Węgierski
- Chleb Orkiszowy
- Chleb Ziołowy
- Chleb Góralski
- Chleb Na Drożdżach
- Chleb Na Mące Tylżyckiej
- Chleb Na Mące Różnej
- Chleb Pszenno-Żytni Na Zakwasie
- Chleb Z Płatkami Owsianymi
- Chleb Na Maślance
- Chleb Wyjątkowy
- Chleb Wypełniony Serem
- Chleb Z Bakaliami
- Chleb Wiejski Żytni
- Chleb Drożdżowy
- Chleb Czosnkowy
- Chleb Z Dynią
- Chleb Na Miodzie
- Chleb Świąteczny
- Chleb Z Białym Serem
- Chleb Bezglutenowy

- **Chleb Maślankowy**
- **Chleb Z Marcepanem**
- **Chleb Z Cebulą**
- **Chleb Żytni Na Zakwasie**
- **Chleb Z Siemieniem Lniany**
- **Chleb Tarty**
- **Chleb Miodowy**
- **Chleb Góralski Żytni**
- **Chleb Na Wodzie**
- **Chleb Z Orzechami**
- **Chleb Na Mące Przemysłowej**
- **Chleb Na Zakwasie Żytnim**
- **Chleb Z Kiełbasą**
- **Chleb Na Owsianych Płatkach**
- **Chleb Z Rodzynkami**
- **Chleb Z Chrzanem**
- **Chleb Wiejski Z Ziołami**
- **Chleb Z Papryką**

Chleb Wiejski

Ingredients:

- 500g (4 cups) all-purpose flour
- 300ml (1 ¼ cups) warm water
- 7g (1 packet) active dry yeast
- 10g (2 teaspoons) salt
- 1 tablespoon sugar (optional, to help activate the yeast)
- 2 tablespoons olive oil or melted butter (optional, for added richness)
- 1 tablespoon caraway seeds (optional, for flavor)

Instructions:

1. **Prepare the Dough:**
    - **Activate the Yeast:** In a small bowl, dissolve the yeast (and sugar, if using) in warm water. Let it sit for about 5 minutes until frothy.
    - **Mix Ingredients:** In a large bowl, combine the flour and salt. Make a well in the center.
    - **Combine:** Pour the yeast mixture and olive oil (if using) into the well of the flour. Mix until the dough starts to come together.
    - **Knead:** Turn the dough out onto a floured surface and knead for about 8-10 minutes, until smooth and elastic. If using, fold in the caraway seeds.
2. **First Rise:**
    - Place the dough in a lightly oiled bowl, cover with a damp cloth or plastic wrap, and let it rise in a warm place for about 1-1.5 hours, or until doubled in size.
3. **Shape and Second Rise:**
    - Punch down the dough and shape it into a round loaf or place it in a greased loaf pan.
    - Cover and let it rise for another 30-45 minutes, or until it has risen again and looks puffy.
4. **Preheat Oven:**
    - Preheat your oven to 220°C (425°F).
5. **Bake:**
    - Optionally, make a few shallow cuts on the surface of the dough for a traditional look.
    - Bake for 25-30 minutes, or until the bread is golden brown and sounds hollow when tapped on the bottom.
6. **Cool:**
    - Allow the bread to cool on a wire rack before slicing.

Chleb Wiejski is perfect for pairing with hearty stews, soups, or just enjoyed with a pat of butter. Enjoy the wholesome, rustic flavor of this classic Polish bread!

Chleb Żytni

Ingredients:

For the Rye Sourdough (Starter):

- 100g (¾ cup) rye flour
- 100ml (⅓ cup + 1 tablespoon) warm water
- 1 teaspoon sugar or honey (optional, to help the fermentation)

For the Bread Dough:

- 300g (2 ½ cups) rye flour
- 200g (1 ½ cups) all-purpose flour
- 300ml (1 ¼ cups) warm water
- 200g (about ¾ cup) active rye sourdough starter (prepared in advance)
- 10g (2 teaspoons) salt
- 1 tablespoon caraway seeds (optional, for flavor)
- 1 tablespoon honey (optional, for a touch of sweetness)

Instructions:

1. **Prepare the Rye Sourdough:**
   - In a bowl, combine the rye flour, warm water, and sugar or honey (if using).
   - Cover with a cloth and let it sit at room temperature for 24 hours. The mixture should become bubbly and slightly sour.
2. **Prepare the Dough:**
   - **Mix Ingredients:** In a large bowl, combine the rye flour, all-purpose flour, and salt. Make a well in the center.
   - **Combine:** Add the rye sourdough starter, warm water, and honey (if using) into the well of the flour mixture. Mix until combined.
   - **Knead:** The dough will be quite sticky. You can mix it with a spoon or spatula until well combined; there's no need for extensive kneading as rye dough is typically denser.
3. **First Rise:**
   - Transfer the dough to a lightly greased or floured bowl, cover with a damp cloth or plastic wrap, and let it rise in a warm place for about 1-1.5 hours, or until it has roughly doubled in size.
4. **Shape and Second Rise:**
   - Punch down the dough and transfer it to a greased loaf pan or shape it into a round loaf and place it on a baking sheet.
   - Cover and let it rise for another 45 minutes to 1 hour, or until it has risen again and looks puffy.
5. **Preheat Oven:**

    - Preheat your oven to 220°C (425°F).
6. **Bake:**
    - Optionally, sprinkle the top of the dough with a little extra rye flour or caraway seeds before baking.
    - Bake for 35-40 minutes, or until the bread is dark brown and sounds hollow when tapped on the bottom.
7. **Cool:**
    - Allow the bread to cool completely on a wire rack before slicing.

Chleb Żytni has a distinctive, tangy flavor from the rye flour and sourdough starter. It's excellent with hearty soups, stews, or simply with butter and cheese. Enjoy this flavorful and satisfying Polish bread!

Chleb Pszenno-Żytni

Ingredients:

For the Rye Sourdough (Starter):

- 100g (¾ cup) rye flour
- 100ml (⅓ cup + 1 tablespoon) warm water
- 1 teaspoon sugar or honey (optional, to help the fermentation)

For the Bread Dough:

- 300g (2 ½ cups) rye flour
- 200g (1 ½ cups) all-purpose flour
- 300ml (1 ¼ cups) warm water
- 200g (about ¾ cup) active rye sourdough starter (prepared in advance)
- 10g (2 teaspoons) salt
- 1 tablespoon caraway seeds (optional, for flavor)
- 1 tablespoon honey (optional, for a touch of sweetness)

Instructions:

1. **Prepare the Rye Sourdough:**
   - In a bowl, combine the rye flour, warm water, and sugar or honey (if using).
   - Cover with a cloth and let it sit at room temperature for 24 hours. The mixture should become bubbly and slightly sour.
2. **Prepare the Dough:**
   - **Mix Ingredients:** In a large bowl, combine the rye flour, all-purpose flour, and salt. Make a well in the center.
   - **Combine:** Add the rye sourdough starter, warm water, and honey (if using) into the well of the flour mixture. Mix until combined.
   - **Knead:** The dough will be quite sticky. You can mix it with a spoon or spatula until well combined; there's no need for extensive kneading as rye dough is typically denser.
3. **First Rise:**
   - Transfer the dough to a lightly greased or floured bowl, cover with a damp cloth or plastic wrap, and let it rise in a warm place for about 1-1.5 hours, or until it has roughly doubled in size.
4. **Shape and Second Rise:**
   - Punch down the dough and transfer it to a greased loaf pan or shape it into a round loaf and place it on a baking sheet.
   - Cover and let it rise for another 45 minutes to 1 hour, or until it has risen again and looks puffy.
5. **Preheat Oven:**

        - Preheat your oven to 220°C (425°F).
6. **Bake:**
        - Optionally, sprinkle the top of the dough with a little extra rye flour or caraway seeds before baking.
        - Bake for 35-40 minutes, or until the bread is dark brown and sounds hollow when tapped on the bottom.
7. **Cool:**
        - Allow the bread to cool completely on a wire rack before slicing.

Chleb Żytni has a distinctive, tangy flavor from the rye flour and sourdough starter. It's excellent with hearty soups, stews, or simply with butter and cheese. Enjoy this flavorful and satisfying Polish bread!

Chleb Rzemieślniczy

Ingredients:

- 500g (4 cups) all-purpose flour
- 300ml (1 ¼ cups) warm water
- 7g (1 packet) active dry yeast
- 10g (2 teaspoons) salt
- 2 tablespoons olive oil (optional, for added richness)
- 1 tablespoon honey or sugar (optional, to help activate the yeast)
- Optional: 1 tablespoon of mixed seeds (like sunflower, flax, or sesame) for topping

Instructions:

1. **Prepare the Dough:**
   - **Activate the Yeast:** In a small bowl, dissolve the yeast (and honey or sugar, if using) in warm water. Let it sit for about 5 minutes until it becomes frothy.
   - **Mix Ingredients:** In a large bowl, combine the flour and salt. Make a well in the center.
   - **Combine:** Pour the yeast mixture and olive oil (if using) into the well of the flour. Mix until the dough starts to come together.
   - **Knead:** Turn the dough out onto a floured surface and knead for about 8-10 minutes, until smooth and elastic.
2. **First Rise:**
   - Place the dough in a lightly oiled bowl, cover with a damp cloth or plastic wrap, and let it rise in a warm place for about 1-1.5 hours, or until doubled in size.
3. **Shape and Second Rise:**
   - Punch down the dough and shape it into a round or oval loaf.
   - Place it on a parchment-lined or lightly floured baking sheet.
   - Cover and let it rise for another 30-45 minutes, or until puffy.
4. **Preheat Oven:**
   - Preheat your oven to 220°C (425°F).
5. **Bake:**
   - Optionally, sprinkle the top of the loaf with mixed seeds before baking.
   - Bake for 25-30 minutes, or until the bread is golden brown and sounds hollow when tapped on the bottom.
6. **Cool:**
   - Allow the bread to cool on a wire rack before slicing.

Chleb Rzemieślniczy is known for its crusty exterior and soft, airy interior. It's perfect for serving with a variety of dishes or enjoying with butter and cheese. Enjoy your artisanal Polish bread!

Chleb Tattarski

Ingredients:

- 250g (2 cups) rye flour
- 250g (2 cups) all-purpose flour
- 300ml (1 ¼ cups) warm water
- 7g (1 packet) active dry yeast
- 10g (2 teaspoons) salt
- 1 tablespoon honey or sugar (optional, to help activate the yeast)
- 2 tablespoons olive oil (optional, for added richness)
- 1 tablespoon caraway seeds or cumin seeds (optional, for flavor)

Instructions:

1. **Prepare the Dough:**
   - **Activate the Yeast:** In a small bowl, dissolve the yeast (and honey or sugar, if using) in warm water. Let it sit for about 5 minutes until it becomes frothy.
   - **Mix Ingredients:** In a large bowl, combine the rye flour, all-purpose flour, and salt. Make a well in the center.
   - **Combine:** Pour the yeast mixture and olive oil (if using) into the well of the flour mixture. Mix until the dough starts to come together. If using, fold in the caraway or cumin seeds.
   - **Knead:** Turn the dough out onto a floured surface and knead for about 8-10 minutes, until smooth and elastic.
2. **First Rise:**
   - Place the dough in a lightly oiled bowl, cover with a damp cloth or plastic wrap, and let it rise in a warm place for about 1-1.5 hours, or until doubled in size.
3. **Shape and Second Rise:**
   - Punch down the dough and shape it into a round or oval loaf.
   - Place it on a parchment-lined or lightly floured baking sheet.
   - Cover and let it rise for another 30-45 minutes, or until puffy.
4. **Preheat Oven:**
   - Preheat your oven to 220°C (425°F).
5. **Bake:**
   - Optionally, you can make a few shallow cuts on the surface of the dough for a traditional look.
   - Bake for 30-35 minutes, or until the bread is deep brown and sounds hollow when tapped on the bottom.
6. **Cool:**
   - Allow the bread to cool on a wire rack before slicing.

Chleb Tattarski has a rich, earthy flavor thanks to the rye flour and optional seeds. It's excellent with hearty soups or stews and makes a satisfying addition to any meal. Enjoy your Tatar bread!

Chleb Grahamski

Ingredients:

- 500g (4 cups) graham flour or whole wheat flour
- 300ml (1 ¼ cups) warm water
- 7g (1 packet) active dry yeast
- 10g (2 teaspoons) salt
- 2 tablespoons honey or molasses (for sweetness and better texture)
- 2 tablespoons olive oil or melted butter (optional, for added richness)
- 1 tablespoon caraway seeds or sunflower seeds (optional, for added flavor)

Instructions:

1. **Prepare the Dough:**
    - **Activate the Yeast:** In a small bowl, dissolve the yeast and honey (or molasses) in warm water. Let it sit for about 5 minutes until it becomes frothy.
    - **Mix Ingredients:** In a large bowl, combine the graham flour (or whole wheat flour) and salt. Make a well in the center.
    - **Combine:** Pour the yeast mixture and olive oil (if using) into the well of the flour. Mix until the dough starts to come together. If using, fold in the caraway seeds or sunflower seeds.
    - **Knead:** Turn the dough out onto a floured surface and knead for about 8-10 minutes, until smooth and elastic.
2. **First Rise:**
    - Place the dough in a lightly oiled bowl, cover with a damp cloth or plastic wrap, and let it rise in a warm place for about 1-1.5 hours, or until doubled in size.
3. **Shape and Second Rise:**
    - Punch down the dough and shape it into a loaf or place it in a greased loaf pan.
    - Cover and let it rise for another 30-45 minutes, or until it has risen again and looks puffy.
4. **Preheat Oven:**
    - Preheat your oven to 220°C (425°F).
5. **Bake:**
    - Optionally, sprinkle the top of the loaf with a little extra graham flour or seeds before baking.
    - Bake for 30-35 minutes, or until the bread is deep brown and sounds hollow when tapped on the bottom.
6. **Cool:**
    - Allow the bread to cool on a wire rack before slicing.

Chleb Grahamski offers a hearty and wholesome flavor that pairs well with a variety of toppings and spreads. It's perfect for enjoying with soups, stews, or simply with a bit of butter. Enjoy baking and savoring this traditional Polish bread!

Chleb Słodowy

Ingredients:

- 500g (4 cups) all-purpose flour
- 300ml (1 ¼ cups) warm water
- 7g (1 packet) active dry yeast
- 10g (2 teaspoons) salt
- 2 tablespoons malt extract or malted barley flour (for a malty flavor)
- 2 tablespoons honey or brown sugar (optional, for added sweetness)
- 2 tablespoons olive oil or melted butter (optional, for richness)

Instructions:

1. **Prepare the Dough:**
    - **Activate the Yeast:** In a small bowl, dissolve the yeast and honey (or brown sugar) in warm water. Let it sit for about 5 minutes until it becomes frothy.
    - **Mix Ingredients:** In a large bowl, combine the flour, salt, and malt extract (or malted barley flour). Make a well in the center.
    - **Combine:** Pour the yeast mixture and olive oil (if using) into the well of the flour. Mix until the dough starts to come together.
    - **Knead:** Turn the dough out onto a floured surface and knead for about 8-10 minutes, until smooth and elastic.
2. **First Rise:**
    - Place the dough in a lightly oiled bowl, cover with a damp cloth or plastic wrap, and let it rise in a warm place for about 1-1.5 hours, or until doubled in size.
3. **Shape and Second Rise:**
    - Punch down the dough and shape it into a loaf or place it in a greased loaf pan.
    - Cover and let it rise for another 30-45 minutes, or until it has risen again and looks puffy.
4. **Preheat Oven:**
    - Preheat your oven to 220°C (425°F).
5. **Bake:**
    - Optionally, you can sprinkle the top of the loaf with a little flour before baking.
    - Bake for 30-35 minutes, or until the bread is dark brown and sounds hollow when tapped on the bottom.
6. **Cool:**
    - Allow the bread to cool on a wire rack before slicing.

Chleb Słodowy's unique malty flavor makes it a delightful choice for sandwiches or as an accompaniment to hearty dishes. Enjoy the rich taste of this traditional Polish bread!

Chleb Na Zakwasie

Ingredients:

For the Sourdough Starter:

- 100g (¾ cup) rye flour
- 100ml (⅓ cup + 1 tablespoon) warm water
- 1 teaspoon honey or sugar (optional, to help fermentation)

For the Bread Dough:

- 300g (2 ½ cups) all-purpose flour
- 200g (1 ½ cups) rye flour
- 300ml (1 ¼ cups) warm water
- 200g (about ¾ cup) active sourdough starter (prepared in advance)
- 10g (2 teaspoons) salt
- 1 tablespoon caraway seeds (optional, for added flavor)

Instructions:

1. **Prepare the Sourdough Starter:**
   - In a bowl, mix the rye flour and warm water. Add honey or sugar if using.
   - Cover loosely with a cloth and let it sit at room temperature for 24 hours. The mixture should become bubbly and slightly sour.
2. **Prepare the Dough:**
   - **Mix Ingredients:** In a large bowl, combine the all-purpose flour, rye flour, and salt. Make a well in the center.
   - **Combine:** Add the sourdough starter and warm water into the well. Mix until the dough starts to come together. If using, fold in the caraway seeds.
   - **Knead:** Turn the dough onto a floured surface and knead for about 8-10 minutes, until smooth and elastic.
3. **First Rise:**
   - Place the dough in a lightly oiled bowl, cover with a damp cloth or plastic wrap, and let it rise in a warm place for about 1-1.5 hours, or until doubled in size.
4. **Shape and Second Rise:**
   - Punch down the dough and shape it into a loaf or place it in a greased loaf pan.
   - Cover and let it rise for another 45 minutes to 1 hour, or until puffy.
5. **Preheat Oven:**
   - Preheat your oven to 220°C (425°F).
6. **Bake:**
   - Optionally, make a few shallow cuts on the surface of the dough for a traditional look.

- Bake for 35-40 minutes, or until the bread is dark brown and sounds hollow when tapped on the bottom.
7. **Cool:**
    - Allow the bread to cool on a wire rack before slicing.

Chleb Na Zakwasie's robust flavor and chewy texture make it ideal for a variety of dishes. Enjoy this classic Polish sourdough bread with soups, stews, or as a hearty sandwich base!

Chleb Kukurydziany

Ingredients:

- 250g (2 cups) cornmeal
- 250g (2 cups) all-purpose flour
- 300ml (1 ¼ cups) warm water or milk
- 7g (1 packet) active dry yeast
- 10g (2 teaspoons) salt
- 2 tablespoons sugar or honey (optional, for sweetness)
- 2 tablespoons olive oil or melted butter (for added richness)
- 1 egg (optional, for a richer crumb)
- 1 teaspoon baking powder (optional, for extra lift)

Instructions:

1. **Prepare the Dough:**
   - **Activate the Yeast:** In a small bowl, dissolve the yeast and sugar (if using) in warm water or milk. Let it sit for about 5 minutes until it becomes frothy.
   - **Mix Ingredients:** In a large bowl, combine the cornmeal, all-purpose flour, salt, and baking powder (if using). Make a well in the center.
   - **Combine:** Pour the yeast mixture, olive oil (or melted butter), and egg (if using) into the well. Mix until the dough starts to come together. The dough may be a bit sticky due to the cornmeal.
   - **Knead:** Turn the dough out onto a floured surface and knead for about 5-8 minutes, until it's smooth and elastic.
2. **First Rise:**
   - Place the dough in a lightly oiled bowl, cover with a damp cloth or plastic wrap, and let it rise in a warm place for about 1 hour, or until doubled in size.
3. **Shape and Second Rise:**
   - Punch down the dough and shape it into a loaf or place it in a greased loaf pan.
   - Cover and let it rise for another 30-45 minutes, or until it has risen again and looks puffy.
4. **Preheat Oven:**
   - Preheat your oven to 220°C (425°F).
5. **Bake:**
   - Optionally, sprinkle the top of the loaf with a little extra cornmeal for a rustic look.
   - Bake for 30-35 minutes, or until the bread is golden brown and sounds hollow when tapped on the bottom.
6. **Cool:**
   - Allow the bread to cool on a wire rack before slicing.

Chleb Kukurydziany's unique texture and flavor make it a wonderful accompaniment to soups, stews, or as a side with various dishes. Enjoy this delightful Polish cornbread fresh from the oven!

Chleb Miejski

Ingredients:

- 500g (4 cups) all-purpose flour
- 300ml (1 ¼ cups) warm water
- 7g (1 packet) active dry yeast
- 10g (2 teaspoons) salt
- 2 tablespoons olive oil or melted butter (for richness)
- 1 tablespoon sugar (optional, to help activate the yeast)
- 1 tablespoon milk powder (optional, for added softness)

Instructions:

1. **Prepare the Dough:**
    - **Activate the Yeast:** In a small bowl, dissolve the yeast and sugar (if using) in warm water. Let it sit for about 5 minutes until it becomes frothy.
    - **Mix Ingredients:** In a large bowl, combine the flour, salt, and milk powder (if using). Make a well in the center.
    - **Combine:** Pour the yeast mixture and olive oil (or melted butter) into the well. Mix until the dough starts to come together.
    - **Knead:** Turn the dough out onto a floured surface and knead for about 8-10 minutes, until smooth and elastic.
2. **First Rise:**
    - Place the dough in a lightly oiled bowl, cover with a damp cloth or plastic wrap, and let it rise in a warm place for about 1-1.5 hours, or until doubled in size.
3. **Shape and Second Rise:**
    - Punch down the dough and shape it into a loaf or place it in a greased loaf pan.
    - Cover and let it rise for another 30-45 minutes, or until puffy.
4. **Preheat Oven:**
    - Preheat your oven to 220°C (425°F).
5. **Bake:**
    - Optionally, make a few shallow cuts on the surface of the dough for a traditional look.
    - Bake for 25-30 minutes, or until the bread is golden brown and sounds hollow when tapped on the bottom.
6. **Cool:**
    - Allow the bread to cool on a wire rack before slicing.

Chleb Miejski is ideal for a wide range of uses, from sandwiches to accompanying soups and salads. Enjoy this versatile and classic Polish bread!

Chleb Ziemniaczany

Ingredients:

- 1 cup mashed potatoes
- 1 cup warm milk
- 1/4 cup melted butter
- 1/4 cup sugar
- 1 tablespoon yeast
- 1 teaspoon salt
- 3-4 cups all-purpose flour

Instructions:

1. Combine warm milk, sugar, and yeast in a bowl. Let sit for 5-10 minutes until frothy.
2. Mix in mashed potatoes and melted butter.
3. Gradually add flour and salt, mixing until a soft dough forms.
4. Knead for 5-7 minutes until smooth.
5. Let rise in a warm place for 1-2 hours or until doubled in size.
6. Shape the dough and place it in a greased loaf pan. Let rise again for 30 minutes.
7. Bake at 375°F (190°C) for 30-35 minutes, until golden brown.

Enjoy your potato bread!

Chleb Węgierski

Ingredients:

- 2 cups warm water
- 1 tablespoon sugar
- 2 tablespoons active dry yeast
- 1/4 cup vegetable oil
- 1 tablespoon salt
- 5 cups all-purpose flour (approximately)
- 1 tablespoon caraway seeds (optional)

Instructions:

1. **Activate the Yeast:**
    - In a small bowl, combine warm water and sugar. Stir to dissolve the sugar.
    - Sprinkle the yeast over the water. Let it sit for about 5-10 minutes until it becomes frothy.
2. **Prepare the Dough:**
    - In a large mixing bowl, combine the activated yeast mixture with oil and salt.
    - Gradually add flour, one cup at a time, mixing well after each addition.
    - Continue to add flour until the dough pulls away from the sides of the bowl and is manageable.
3. **Knead the Dough:**
    - Turn the dough out onto a floured surface. Knead for about 8-10 minutes, until the dough is smooth and elastic.
    - If using, knead in the caraway seeds at this stage.
4. **First Rise:**
    - Place the dough in a greased bowl, turning it to coat all sides with oil.
    - Cover with a clean cloth or plastic wrap and let it rise in a warm, draft-free area for about 1-1.5 hours, or until doubled in size.
5. **Shape the Loaf:**
    - Punch down the dough to release air bubbles.
    - Turn it out onto a floured surface and shape it into a loaf. Alternatively, you can divide the dough and shape it into smaller loaves.
6. **Second Rise:**
    - Place the shaped dough into greased loaf pans or on a baking sheet.
    - Cover with a cloth and let rise for another 30-45 minutes, until nearly doubled.
7. **Bake:**
    - Preheat your oven to 375°F (190°C).
    - Bake the bread for 30-35 minutes, or until the loaf is golden brown and sounds hollow when tapped on the bottom.

8. **Cool:**
    - Allow the bread to cool on a wire rack before slicing.

Enjoy your Chleb Węgierski with some butter, cheese, or as part of a hearty meal!

Chleb Orkiszowy

Ingredients:

- 3 1/2 cups spelt flour
- 1 1/2 cups warm water
- 2 tablespoons olive oil
- 2 tablespoons honey or maple syrup
- 1 tablespoon active dry yeast
- 1 teaspoon salt
- Optional: 1 tablespoon of flax seeds or sunflower seeds for added texture and flavor

Instructions:

1. **Activate the Yeast:**
    - In a small bowl, combine the warm water and honey (or maple syrup). Stir to dissolve.
    - Sprinkle the yeast over the water and let it sit for 5-10 minutes until it becomes frothy.
2. **Mix the Dough:**
    - In a large bowl, combine the spelt flour and salt.
    - Make a well in the center and pour in the activated yeast mixture and olive oil.
    - Mix until a sticky dough forms. You can add flax seeds or sunflower seeds if you like.
3. **Knead the Dough:**
    - Turn the dough out onto a lightly floured surface and knead for about 5-7 minutes, until it becomes smooth and elastic.
4. **First Rise:**
    - Place the dough in a lightly oiled bowl, turning it around to coat all sides.
    - Cover with a clean cloth or plastic wrap and let it rise in a warm, draft-free area for about 1-1.5 hours, or until doubled in size.
5. **Shape the Loaf:**
    - Punch down the dough to release air bubbles.
    - Shape the dough into a loaf and place it into a greased loaf pan or onto a parchment-lined baking sheet.
6. **Second Rise:**
    - Cover the shaped dough with a cloth and let it rise for another 30-45 minutes, until it has puffed up.
7. **Bake:**
    - Preheat your oven to 375°F (190°C).
    - Bake the bread for 30-35 minutes, or until it's golden brown and sounds hollow when tapped on the bottom.

8. **Cool:**
    - Allow the bread to cool on a wire rack before slicing.

Enjoy your Chleb Orkiszowy fresh out of the oven, or toasted with your favorite toppings!

Chleb Ziołowy

Ingredients:

- 3 1/2 cups all-purpose flour (or bread flour)
- 1 1/2 cups warm water
- 2 tablespoons olive oil
- 2 tablespoons sugar or honey
- 2 tablespoons fresh herbs (such as rosemary, thyme, basil, or parsley), finely chopped
- 1 tablespoon active dry yeast
- 1 teaspoon salt
- Optional: 1/2 teaspoon dried herbs (if you want to enhance the herbal flavor)

Instructions:

1. **Activate the Yeast:**
    - In a small bowl, combine the warm water and sugar (or honey). Stir to dissolve.
    - Sprinkle the yeast over the mixture and let it sit for 5-10 minutes until it becomes frothy.
2. **Mix the Dough:**
    - In a large bowl, combine the flour and salt.
    - Create a well in the center and add the activated yeast mixture and olive oil.
    - Mix until the dough begins to come together. Then add the fresh herbs (and dried herbs, if using).
3. **Knead the Dough:**
    - Turn the dough out onto a floured surface and knead for about 8-10 minutes, until it is smooth and elastic.
4. **First Rise:**
    - Place the dough in a lightly oiled bowl, turning it around to coat all sides with oil.
    - Cover with a clean cloth or plastic wrap and let it rise in a warm, draft-free area for 1-1.5 hours, or until doubled in size.
5. **Shape the Loaf:**
    - Punch down the dough to release the air.
    - Shape the dough into a loaf and place it in a greased loaf pan, or shape it into a round loaf and place it on a parchment-lined baking sheet.
6. **Second Rise:**
    - Cover the shaped dough with a cloth and let it rise for another 30-45 minutes, until it has puffed up.
7. **Bake:**
    - Preheat your oven to 375°F (190°C).
    - Bake the bread for 30-35 minutes, or until it is golden brown and sounds hollow when tapped on the bottom.

8. **Cool:**
    - Allow the bread to cool on a wire rack before slicing.

This Chleb Ziołowy will have a delightful herbal aroma and flavor. Enjoy it fresh or toasted, and feel free to experiment with your favorite herbs!

Chleb Góralski

Ingredients:

- 3 1/2 cups all-purpose flour
- 1 1/2 cups warm water
- 2 tablespoons lard or butter
- 1 tablespoon sugar
- 1 tablespoon active dry yeast
- 1 teaspoon salt
- 1 teaspoon caraway seeds (optional)

Instructions:

1. **Activate the Yeast:**
   - In a small bowl, combine warm water and sugar. Stir to dissolve.
   - Sprinkle the yeast over the mixture and let it sit for 5-10 minutes until it becomes frothy.
2. **Mix the Dough:**
   - In a large bowl, combine flour and salt (and caraway seeds if using).
   - Make a well in the center and pour in the activated yeast mixture and melted lard (or butter).
   - Mix until a dough forms.
3. **Knead the Dough:**
   - Turn the dough out onto a floured surface and knead for 8-10 minutes, until it is smooth and elastic.
4. **First Rise:**
   - Place the dough in a lightly oiled bowl, turning it to coat with oil.
   - Cover with a cloth and let it rise in a warm, draft-free area for 1-1.5 hours, or until doubled in size.
5. **Shape the Loaf:**
   - Punch down the dough to release the air.
   - Shape into a round loaf or place into a greased loaf pan.
6. **Second Rise:**
   - Cover the shaped dough and let it rise for another 30-45 minutes.
7. **Bake:**
   - Preheat your oven to 375°F (190°C).
   - Bake for 30-35 minutes, until the bread is golden brown and sounds hollow when tapped on the bottom.
8. **Cool:**
   - Allow the bread to cool on a wire rack before slicing.

This bread has a hearty, dense texture perfect for pairing with hearty meals. Enjoy!

Chleb Na Drożdżach

Ingredients:

- 3 1/2 cups all-purpose flour
- 1 1/2 cups warm water (110°F or 45°C)
- 2 tablespoons sugar
- 2 tablespoons active dry yeast
- 2 tablespoons olive oil (or melted butter)
- 1 teaspoon salt
- Optional: 1 tablespoon of any seeds or herbs for extra flavor

Instructions:

1. **Activate the Yeast:**
   - In a small bowl, combine the warm water and sugar. Stir to dissolve.
   - Sprinkle the yeast over the mixture and let it sit for 5-10 minutes, until it becomes frothy.
2. **Mix the Dough:**
   - In a large mixing bowl, combine the flour and salt.
   - Create a well in the center and pour in the activated yeast mixture and olive oil (or melted butter).
   - Mix until the dough starts to come together. If you're using seeds or herbs, you can add them at this stage.
3. **Knead the Dough:**
   - Turn the dough out onto a floured surface and knead for about 8-10 minutes, until it becomes smooth and elastic.
4. **First Rise:**
   - Place the dough in a lightly oiled bowl, turning it to coat all sides with oil.
   - Cover with a clean cloth or plastic wrap and let it rise in a warm, draft-free area for 1-1.5 hours, or until doubled in size.
5. **Shape the Loaf:**
   - Punch down the dough to release air bubbles.
   - Shape the dough into a loaf or divide it into smaller portions for rolls. Place it in a greased loaf pan or on a parchment-lined baking sheet.
6. **Second Rise:**
   - Cover the shaped dough with a cloth and let it rise for another 30-45 minutes, until it has puffed up.
7. **Bake:**
   - Preheat your oven to 375°F (190°C).
   - Bake the bread for 30-35 minutes, or until it's golden brown and sounds hollow when tapped on the bottom.

8. **Cool:**
    - Allow the bread to cool on a wire rack before slicing.

This yeast bread is perfect for sandwiches, toast, or as an accompaniment to soups and stews. Enjoy the fresh, homemade goodness!

Chleb Na Mące Tylżyckiej

Ingredients:

- 3 1/2 cups Tylżycka flour (or substitute with high-quality all-purpose flour)
- 1 1/2 cups warm water
- 2 tablespoons sugar
- 2 tablespoons active dry yeast
- 2 tablespoons olive oil or melted butter
- 1 teaspoon salt
- Optional: 1 tablespoon of caraway seeds or dried herbs for extra flavor

Instructions:

1. **Activate the Yeast:**
   - In a small bowl, combine warm water and sugar. Stir to dissolve.
   - Sprinkle the yeast over the mixture and let it sit for 5-10 minutes, until frothy.
2. **Mix the Dough:**
   - In a large mixing bowl, combine the Tylżycka flour and salt.
   - Make a well in the center and add the activated yeast mixture and olive oil (or melted butter).
   - Mix until a dough starts to form. If using, incorporate caraway seeds or herbs.
3. **Knead the Dough:**
   - Turn the dough out onto a floured surface and knead for about 8-10 minutes, until smooth and elastic.
4. **First Rise:**
   - Place the dough in a lightly oiled bowl, turning to coat all sides.
   - Cover with a cloth and let it rise in a warm, draft-free area for 1-1.5 hours, or until doubled in size.
5. **Shape the Loaf:**
   - Punch down the dough and shape it into a loaf or divide it for smaller rolls.
   - Place in a greased loaf pan or on a parchment-lined baking sheet.
6. **Second Rise:**
   - Cover and let the shaped dough rise for another 30-45 minutes, until puffy.
7. **Bake:**
   - Preheat your oven to 375°F (190°C).
   - Bake for 30-35 minutes, or until golden brown and sounding hollow when tapped.
8. **Cool:**
   - Let the bread cool on a wire rack before slicing.

This bread will have a hearty texture and a rich flavor from the Tylżycka flour. Enjoy!

Chleb Na Mące Różnej

Ingredients:

- 2 cups all-purpose flour
- 1 cup whole wheat flour
- 1 cup rye flour
- 1 1/2 cups warm water
- 2 tablespoons sugar or honey
- 2 tablespoons active dry yeast
- 2 tablespoons olive oil or melted butter
- 1 teaspoon salt
- Optional: 1 tablespoon of seeds (such as sunflower or flax) or herbs for added texture and flavor

Instructions:

1. **Activate the Yeast:**
    - In a small bowl, combine warm water and sugar (or honey). Stir to dissolve.
    - Sprinkle the yeast over the mixture and let it sit for 5-10 minutes, until it becomes frothy.
2. **Mix the Dough:**
    - In a large mixing bowl, combine all-purpose flour, whole wheat flour, rye flour, and salt.
    - Make a well in the center and add the activated yeast mixture and olive oil (or melted butter).
    - Mix until a dough forms. If using seeds or herbs, add them to the dough at this stage.
3. **Knead the Dough:**
    - Turn the dough out onto a floured surface and knead for about 8-10 minutes, until the dough is smooth and elastic.
4. **First Rise:**
    - Place the dough in a lightly oiled bowl, turning it to coat all sides.
    - Cover with a cloth and let it rise in a warm, draft-free area for 1-1.5 hours, or until doubled in size.
5. **Shape the Loaf:**
    - Punch down the dough to release air bubbles.
    - Shape the dough into a loaf or divide it into smaller portions for rolls. Place it in a greased loaf pan or on a parchment-lined baking sheet.
6. **Second Rise:**
    - Cover the shaped dough and let it rise for another 30-45 minutes, until puffy.
7. **Bake:**

- Preheat your oven to 375°F (190°C).
- Bake the bread for 30-35 minutes, or until it is golden brown and sounds hollow when tapped on the bottom.

8. **Cool:**
    - Allow the bread to cool on a wire rack before slicing.

This bread, with its combination of flours, will have a robust and hearty flavor with a pleasant texture. Enjoy it fresh or toasted, with your favorite spreads or as an accompaniment to meals!

Chleb Pszenno-Żytni Na Zakwasie

Ingredients:

For the Sourdough Starter:

- 1/2 cup rye flour
- 1/2 cup warm water
- 1 tablespoon honey or sugar (optional)

For the Bread:

- 1 cup active sourdough starter
- 2 cups all-purpose flour
- 1 cup rye flour
- 1 1/2 cups warm water
- 1 tablespoon salt
- Optional: 1 tablespoon caraway seeds or sunflower seeds

Instructions:

1. **Prepare the Sourdough Starter (if not using an existing one):**
    - Mix the rye flour and warm water in a bowl.
    - Add honey or sugar if using.
    - Cover loosely and let it sit at room temperature for 24 hours. Feed the starter daily with equal parts flour and water until it's bubbly and active (usually 3-5 days).
2. **Prepare the Dough:**
    - In a large mixing bowl, combine the all-purpose flour, rye flour, and salt.
    - Add the active sourdough starter and warm water.
    - Mix until a shaggy dough forms. If using seeds, add them now.
3. **Knead the Dough:**
    - Turn the dough onto a floured surface and knead for about 8-10 minutes until smooth and elastic.
4. **First Rise:**
    - Place the dough in a lightly oiled bowl, turning it to coat all sides.
    - Cover with a cloth or plastic wrap and let it rise at room temperature for 4-6 hours, or until doubled in size.
5. **Shape the Loaf:**
    - Punch down the dough and shape it into a loaf or divide into smaller portions for rolls.
    - Place in a greased loaf pan or on a parchment-lined baking sheet.
6. **Second Rise:**

- Cover and let rise for another 1-2 hours, until puffy.
7. **Bake:**
    - Preheat your oven to 375°F (190°C).
    - Bake for 30-35 minutes, or until the bread is golden brown and sounds hollow when tapped.
8. **Cool:**
    - Allow the bread to cool on a wire rack before slicing.

Enjoy the hearty, tangy flavor of your homemade sourdough rye-wheat bread!

Chleb Z Płatkami Owsianymi

Ingredients:

- 2 1/2 cups all-purpose flour
- 1 cup rolled oats
- 1 cup warm water
- 1/2 cup milk
- 1/4 cup honey or maple syrup
- 2 tablespoons olive oil
- 2 tablespoons active dry yeast
- 1 teaspoon salt
- Optional: 1/2 cup of oat flakes for topping

Instructions:

1. **Activate the Yeast:**
    - In a small bowl, combine warm water and honey or maple syrup. Stir to dissolve.
    - Sprinkle the yeast over the mixture and let it sit for 5-10 minutes, until frothy.
2. **Mix the Dough:**
    - In a large bowl, combine flour, oats, and salt.
    - Make a well in the center and add the activated yeast mixture, milk, and olive oil.
    - Mix until a dough forms.
3. **Knead the Dough:**
    - Turn the dough out onto a floured surface and knead for about 8 minutes, until smooth and elastic.
4. **First Rise:**
    - Place the dough in a lightly oiled bowl, turning to coat all sides.
    - Cover with a cloth and let it rise in a warm, draft-free area for 1-1.5 hours, or until doubled in size.
5. **Shape the Loaf:**
    - Punch down the dough and shape it into a loaf.
    - Place it in a greased loaf pan or on a parchment-lined baking sheet.
6. **Second Rise:**
    - Cover and let the shaped dough rise for another 30-45 minutes.
    - If desired, sprinkle additional oat flakes on top of the loaf before baking.
7. **Bake:**
    - Preheat your oven to 375°F (190°C).
    - Bake for 30-35 minutes, or until the bread is golden brown and sounds hollow when tapped.
8. **Cool:**
    - Allow the bread to cool on a wire rack before slicing.

This oatmeal bread is great for sandwiches or simply toasted with a bit of butter. Enjoy the wholesome goodness!

Chleb Na Maślance

Ingredients:

- 3 1/2 cups all-purpose flour
- 1 1/2 cups buttermilk
- 1/4 cup melted butter
- 2 tablespoons sugar
- 2 tablespoons active dry yeast
- 1 teaspoon salt
- Optional: 1 tablespoon sesame or poppy seeds for topping

Instructions:

1. **Activate the Yeast:**
    - In a small bowl, combine warm buttermilk (about 110°F or 45°C) and sugar. Stir to dissolve.
    - Sprinkle the yeast over the mixture and let it sit for 5-10 minutes, until frothy.
2. **Mix the Dough:**
    - In a large mixing bowl, combine the flour and salt.
    - Make a well in the center and add the activated yeast mixture and melted butter.
    - Mix until a dough forms.
3. **Knead the Dough:**
    - Turn the dough onto a floured surface and knead for about 8 minutes, until smooth and elastic.
4. **First Rise:**
    - Place the dough in a lightly oiled bowl, turning to coat all sides.
    - Cover with a cloth and let it rise in a warm, draft-free area for 1-1.5 hours, or until doubled in size.
5. **Shape the Loaf:**
    - Punch down the dough and shape it into a loaf.
    - Place it in a greased loaf pan or on a parchment-lined baking sheet. If desired, sprinkle sesame or poppy seeds on top.
6. **Second Rise:**
    - Cover and let the dough rise for another 30-45 minutes.
7. **Bake:**
    - Preheat your oven to 375°F (190°C).
    - Bake for 30-35 minutes, or until the bread is golden brown and sounds hollow when tapped.
8. **Cool:**
    - Allow the bread to cool on a wire rack before slicing.

Enjoy the moist and flavorful goodness of your buttermilk bread!

Chleb Wyjątkowy

Ingredients:

- 2 cups all-purpose flour
- 1 cup whole wheat flour
- 1/2 cup rye flour
- 1 cup warm water
- 1/2 cup milk
- 1/4 cup honey
- 2 tablespoons olive oil
- 2 tablespoons active dry yeast
- 1 teaspoon salt
- 1/4 cup sunflower seeds
- 1/4 cup chopped nuts (e.g., walnuts or pecans)
- 1/4 cup dried fruit (e.g., raisins or dried apricots), chopped

Instructions:

1. **Activate the Yeast:**
   - In a small bowl, combine warm water and honey. Stir to dissolve.
   - Sprinkle the yeast over the mixture and let it sit for 5-10 minutes, until frothy.
2. **Mix the Dough:**
   - In a large mixing bowl, combine the all-purpose flour, whole wheat flour, rye flour, and salt.
   - Make a well in the center and add the activated yeast mixture, milk, and olive oil.
   - Mix until a dough forms. Fold in sunflower seeds, nuts, and dried fruit.
3. **Knead the Dough:**
   - Turn the dough out onto a floured surface and knead for about 8-10 minutes, until smooth and elastic.
4. **First Rise:**
   - Place the dough in a lightly oiled bowl, turning to coat all sides.
   - Cover with a cloth and let it rise in a warm, draft-free area for 1-1.5 hours, or until doubled in size.
5. **Shape the Loaf:**
   - Punch down the dough and shape it into a loaf or divide into smaller portions for rolls.
   - Place in a greased loaf pan or on a parchment-lined baking sheet.
6. **Second Rise:**
   - Cover and let the dough rise for another 30-45 minutes.
7. **Bake:**
   - Preheat your oven to 375°F (190°C).

- Bake for 30-35 minutes, or until the bread is golden brown and sounds hollow when tapped.
8. **Cool:**
    - Allow the bread to cool on a wire rack before slicing.

This bread's combination of whole grains, seeds, nuts, and dried fruit makes it a delightful and special treat. Enjoy!

Chleb Wypełniony Serem

Ingredients:

For the Bread Dough:

- 3 1/2 cups all-purpose flour
- 1 1/2 cups warm water (110°F or 45°C)
- 2 tablespoons sugar
- 2 tablespoons active dry yeast
- 1/4 cup olive oil
- 1 teaspoon salt

For the Cheese Filling:

- 1 1/2 cups shredded cheese (cheddar, mozzarella, or your favorite cheese)
- 1/2 cup cream cheese, softened
- 1 tablespoon fresh herbs (such as parsley, chives, or thyme), finely chopped (optional)

Instructions:

1. **Activate the Yeast:**
    - In a small bowl, combine warm water and sugar. Stir to dissolve.
    - Sprinkle the yeast over the mixture and let it sit for 5-10 minutes, until frothy.
2. **Mix the Dough:**
    - In a large mixing bowl, combine the flour and salt.
    - Make a well in the center and add the activated yeast mixture and olive oil.
    - Mix until a dough forms.
3. **Knead the Dough:**
    - Turn the dough onto a floured surface and knead for about 8-10 minutes, until smooth and elastic.
4. **First Rise:**
    - Place the dough in a lightly oiled bowl, turning to coat all sides.
    - Cover with a cloth and let it rise in a warm, draft-free area for 1-1.5 hours, or until doubled in size.
5. **Prepare the Cheese Filling:**
    - In a bowl, combine the shredded cheese, cream cheese, and herbs if using. Mix until well combined.
6. **Shape the Bread:**
    - Punch down the dough and turn it out onto a floured surface.
    - Roll out the dough into a rectangle (about 12x16 inches).
    - Spread the cheese mixture evenly over the dough, leaving a small border around the edges.
    - Roll up the dough tightly from one end to the other to form a log.
7. **Second Rise:**
    - Place the rolled dough seam-side down on a greased baking sheet or in a greased loaf pan.

- Cover and let rise for another 30-45 minutes.
8. **Bake:**
    - Preheat your oven to 375°F (190°C).
    - Bake the bread for 25-30 minutes, or until golden brown and the cheese is bubbly.
9. **Cool:**
    - Allow the bread to cool slightly before slicing.

This cheese-stuffed bread is perfect for serving warm and fresh. Enjoy the melty cheese and soft, flavorful bread!

Chleb Z Bakaliami

Ingredients:

- 3 1/2 cups all-purpose flour
- 1 1/2 cups warm water (110°F or 45°C)
- 1/4 cup honey or maple syrup
- 2 tablespoons active dry yeast
- 1/4 cup olive oil or melted butter
- 1 teaspoon salt

For the Filling:

- 1/2 cup chopped dried fruit (such as raisins, apricots, figs, or dates)
- 1/2 cup chopped nuts (such as walnuts, pecans, or almonds)
- 1/4 cup chopped candied fruit (optional)
- 1 tablespoon ground cinnamon (optional, for extra flavor)

Instructions:

1. **Activate the Yeast:**
   - In a small bowl, combine warm water and honey or maple syrup. Stir to dissolve.
   - Sprinkle the yeast over the mixture and let it sit for 5-10 minutes, until frothy.
2. **Mix the Dough:**
   - In a large mixing bowl, combine the flour and salt.
   - Make a well in the center and add the activated yeast mixture and olive oil (or melted butter).
   - Mix until a dough forms.
3. **Knead the Dough:**
   - Turn the dough out onto a floured surface and knead for about 8-10 minutes, until smooth and elastic.
4. **Prepare the Filling:**
   - In a small bowl, combine the chopped dried fruit, nuts, and candied fruit (if using). Toss with ground cinnamon if desired.
5. **Incorporate the Filling:**
   - Punch down the dough and turn it out onto a floured surface.
   - Roll out the dough into a rectangle (about 12x16 inches).
   - Sprinkle the dried fruit and nut mixture evenly over the dough.
   - Roll up the dough tightly from one end to the other to form a log.
6. **Shape the Loaf:**
   - Place the rolled dough seam-side down on a greased baking sheet or in a greased loaf pan.
   - Cover and let rise for another 30-45 minutes.

7. **Bake:**
    - Preheat your oven to 375°F (190°C).
    - Bake the bread for 30-35 minutes, or until golden brown and the bread sounds hollow when tapped.
8. **Cool:**
    - Allow the bread to cool on a wire rack before slicing.

This bread is slightly sweet, packed with the crunch of nuts and the chewiness of dried fruits, making it a delightful treat for any time of day. Enjoy!

Chleb Wiejski Żytni

Ingredients:

- 2 1/2 cups rye flour
- 1 1/2 cups all-purpose flour
- 1 1/2 cups warm water
- 1/4 cup sourdough starter (active) or 1 packet (2 1/4 teaspoons) active dry yeast
- 1 tablespoon sugar or honey
- 2 tablespoons caraway seeds (optional)
- 1 teaspoon salt
- 2 tablespoons olive oil or melted butter

Instructions:

1. **Prepare the Sourdough Starter (if using):**
   - If you're using a sourdough starter, make sure it's active and bubbly. If not, you can use active dry yeast as an alternative.
2. **Activate the Yeast (if using dry yeast):**
   - In a small bowl, combine warm water and sugar or honey. Stir to dissolve.
   - Sprinkle the yeast over the mixture and let it sit for 5-10 minutes, until frothy.
3. **Mix the Dough:**
   - In a large mixing bowl, combine the rye flour, all-purpose flour, salt, and caraway seeds (if using).
   - Make a well in the center and add the activated sourdough starter (or yeast mixture) and olive oil (or melted butter).
   - Mix until a dough forms. Rye dough is typically stickier and denser than wheat dough.
4. **Knead the Dough:**
   - Turn the dough onto a floured surface and knead for about 5-7 minutes. Because rye flour lacks gluten, it won't be as elastic as wheat dough but should be smooth and combined.
5. **First Rise:**
   - Place the dough in a lightly oiled bowl, turning to coat all sides.
   - Cover with a cloth or plastic wrap and let it rise in a warm, draft-free area for 1-1.5 hours, or until doubled in size.
6. **Shape the Loaf:**
   - Punch down the dough to release the air bubbles.
   - Shape the dough into a loaf or round and place it on a greased baking sheet or in a greased loaf pan.
7. **Second Rise:**
   - Cover the shaped dough and let it rise for another 30-45 minutes, or until puffy.

8. **Bake:**
   - Preheat your oven to 375°F (190°C).
   - Bake the bread for 35-40 minutes, or until the crust is dark brown and the bread sounds hollow when tapped.
9. **Cool:**
   - Allow the bread to cool on a wire rack before slicing.

This rye bread is hearty and flavorful, perfect for sandwiches, or served with a bit of butter and cheese. Enjoy the rich, earthy taste of traditional country rye bread!

Chleb Drożdżowy

Ingredients:

- 3 1/2 cups all-purpose flour
- 1 1/2 cups warm water (110°F or 45°C)
- 2 tablespoons sugar
- 2 tablespoons active dry yeast
- 1/4 cup olive oil or melted butter
- 1 teaspoon salt
- Optional: 1 tablespoon sesame seeds or poppy seeds for topping

Instructions:

1. **Activate the Yeast:**
    - In a small bowl, combine warm water and sugar. Stir to dissolve.
    - Sprinkle the yeast over the mixture and let it sit for 5-10 minutes, until frothy.
2. **Mix the Dough:**
    - In a large mixing bowl, combine the flour and salt.
    - Make a well in the center and add the activated yeast mixture and olive oil (or melted butter).
    - Mix until a dough forms. If the dough is too sticky, add a little more flour as needed.
3. **Knead the Dough:**
    - Turn the dough out onto a floured surface and knead for about 8-10 minutes, until smooth and elastic.
4. **First Rise:**
    - Place the dough in a lightly oiled bowl, turning to coat all sides.
    - Cover with a cloth or plastic wrap and let it rise in a warm, draft-free area for 1-1.5 hours, or until doubled in size.
5. **Shape the Loaf:**
    - Punch down the dough to release the air bubbles.
    - Shape the dough into a loaf or divide it into smaller portions for rolls. Place it in a greased loaf pan or on a parchment-lined baking sheet.
    - If using, sprinkle sesame seeds or poppy seeds on top of the loaf.
6. **Second Rise:**
    - Cover the shaped dough and let it rise for another 30-45 minutes, or until puffy.
7. **Bake:**
    - Preheat your oven to 375°F (190°C).
    - Bake the bread for 30-35 minutes, or until golden brown and the bread sounds hollow when tapped.
8. **Cool:**

- Allow the bread to cool on a wire rack before slicing.

This yeast bread is versatile and can be used for sandwiches, toast, or as an accompaniment to any meal. Enjoy the soft, fresh bread with a crispy crust!

Chleb Czosnkowy

Ingredients:

- 1 loaf of French or Italian bread
- 1/2 cup (1 stick) unsalted butter, softened
- 4-6 cloves garlic, minced
- 2 tablespoons fresh parsley, finely chopped (or 1 tablespoon dried parsley)
- 1/4 teaspoon salt
- 1/4 teaspoon black pepper
- Optional: 1/4 cup grated Parmesan cheese

Instructions:

1. **Preheat Oven:**
   - Preheat your oven to 375°F (190°C).
2. **Prepare the Garlic Butter:**
   - In a bowl, mix the softened butter, minced garlic, parsley, salt, and pepper until well combined. If using, stir in the grated Parmesan cheese.
3. **Prepare the Bread:**
   - Slice the loaf of bread in half lengthwise. You can also cut it into smaller pieces or slices if preferred.
4. **Spread the Butter:**
   - Spread the garlic butter mixture evenly over the cut sides of the bread.
5. **Bake:**
   - Place the bread on a baking sheet and bake for 10-15 minutes, or until the edges are golden and the butter is melted.
6. **Optional Broil:**
   - For a crispy top, you can broil the bread for an additional 1-2 minutes, watching closely to avoid burning.
7. **Serve:**
   - Remove from the oven, let cool slightly, and then cut into pieces if needed.

This garlic bread is best served warm and fresh. Enjoy the rich, buttery, and garlicky goodness!

Chleb Z Dynią

Ingredients:

- **For the Bread:**
    - 2 cups all-purpose flour
    - 1 cup whole wheat flour
    - 1 cup canned pumpkin puree (not pumpkin pie filling)
    - 1/2 cup brown sugar
    - 1/2 cup granulated sugar
    - 1/2 cup vegetable oil
    - 1 cup warm water (110°F or 45°C)
    - 2 tablespoons active dry yeast
    - 1 teaspoon salt
    - 1 teaspoon ground cinnamon
    - 1/2 teaspoon ground nutmeg
    - 1/4 teaspoon ground ginger
    - 1/4 teaspoon ground cloves
    - Optional: 1/2 cup chopped nuts or seeds (e.g., walnuts, pecans, sunflower seeds)

Instructions:

1. **Activate the Yeast:**
    - In a small bowl, combine warm water and granulated sugar. Stir to dissolve.
    - Sprinkle the yeast over the mixture and let it sit for 5-10 minutes, until frothy.
2. **Mix the Dough:**
    - In a large mixing bowl, combine the all-purpose flour, whole wheat flour, salt, cinnamon, nutmeg, ginger, and cloves.
    - Make a well in the center and add the activated yeast mixture, pumpkin puree, and vegetable oil.
    - Mix until a dough forms. If using, fold in the chopped nuts or seeds.
3. **Knead the Dough:**
    - Turn the dough onto a floured surface and knead for about 8-10 minutes, until smooth and elastic.
4. **First Rise:**
    - Place the dough in a lightly oiled bowl, turning to coat all sides.
    - Cover with a cloth or plastic wrap and let it rise in a warm, draft-free area for 1-1.5 hours, or until doubled in size.
5. **Shape the Loaf:**
    - Punch down the dough to release air bubbles.
    - Shape the dough into a loaf and place it in a greased loaf pan, or divide into smaller portions for rolls.
6. **Second Rise:**
    - Cover and let the dough rise for another 30-45 minutes, or until puffy.
7. **Bake:**

- Preheat your oven to 375°F (190°C).
- Bake the bread for 30-35 minutes, or until golden brown and the bread sounds hollow when tapped.

8. **Cool:**
   - Allow the bread to cool on a wire rack before slicing.

This pumpkin bread has a lovely, moist texture with a warm, spicy aroma that's perfect for fall. Enjoy it toasted with a bit of butter, or as a delicious accompaniment to soups and stews!

Chleb Na Miodzie

Ingredients:

- **For the Dough:**
    - 3 1/2 cups all-purpose flour
    - 1 1/2 cups warm water (110°F or 45°C)
    - 1/2 cup honey
    - 1/4 cup melted butter or vegetable oil
    - 2 tablespoons active dry yeast
    - 1 teaspoon salt
- **For the Glaze (optional):**
    - 2 tablespoons honey
    - 1 tablespoon water

Instructions:

1. **Activate the Yeast:**
    - In a small bowl, combine warm water and 1/4 cup of honey. Stir to dissolve.
    - Sprinkle the yeast over the mixture and let it sit for 5-10 minutes, until frothy.
2. **Mix the Dough:**
    - In a large mixing bowl, combine the flour and salt.
    - Make a well in the center and add the activated yeast mixture, the remaining honey, and melted butter (or vegetable oil).
    - Mix until a dough forms.
3. **Knead the Dough:**
    - Turn the dough onto a floured surface and knead for about 8-10 minutes, until smooth and elastic.
4. **First Rise:**
    - Place the dough in a lightly oiled bowl, turning to coat all sides.
    - Cover with a cloth or plastic wrap and let it rise in a warm, draft-free area for 1-1.5 hours, or until doubled in size.
5. **Shape the Loaf:**
    - Punch down the dough to release air bubbles.
    - Shape the dough into a loaf and place it in a greased loaf pan, or divide it into smaller portions for rolls.
6. **Second Rise:**
    - Cover and let the dough rise for another 30-45 minutes, or until puffy.
7. **Bake:**
    - Preheat your oven to 375°F (190°C).
    - Bake the bread for 30-35 minutes, or until golden brown and the bread sounds hollow when tapped.

8. **Glaze (Optional):**
    - While the bread is baking, you can prepare the glaze. In a small saucepan, combine 2 tablespoons honey and 1 tablespoon water. Heat over low heat until the honey is liquefied.
    - Brush the glaze over the warm bread as soon as it comes out of the oven for a sweet, shiny finish.
9. **Cool:**
    - Allow the bread to cool on a wire rack before slicing.

This honey bread is slightly sweet with a lovely soft texture, making it a versatile addition to any meal. Enjoy it with a pat of butter or simply on its own!

Chleb Świąteczny

Ingredients:

- **For the Dough:**
    - 3 1/2 cups all-purpose flour
    - 1 cup warm milk (110°F or 45°C)
    - 1/2 cup sugar
    - 1/2 cup unsalted butter, softened
    - 2 large eggs
    - 2 tablespoons active dry yeast
    - 1 teaspoon vanilla extract
    - 1/2 teaspoon salt
    - 1 teaspoon ground cinnamon
    - 1/4 teaspoon ground nutmeg
- **For the Filling (Optional):**
    - 1/2 cup raisins or currants
    - 1/2 cup chopped nuts (e.g., walnuts, almonds)
    - 1/2 cup chopped candied fruit or dried fruit (e.g., apricots, cranberries)
- **For the Glaze (Optional):**
    - 1/4 cup powdered sugar
    - 1-2 tablespoons milk or water

Instructions:

1. **Activate the Yeast:**
    - In a small bowl, combine warm milk and sugar. Stir to dissolve.
    - Sprinkle the yeast over the mixture and let it sit for 5-10 minutes, until frothy.
2. **Mix the Dough:**
    - In a large mixing bowl, combine the flour, cinnamon, nutmeg, and salt.
    - Make a well in the center and add the activated yeast mixture, softened butter, eggs, and vanilla extract.
    - Mix until a dough forms. If using, fold in the raisins, nuts, and candied fruit.
3. **Knead the Dough:**
    - Turn the dough onto a floured surface and knead for about 8-10 minutes, until smooth and elastic.
4. **First Rise:**
    - Place the dough in a lightly oiled bowl, turning to coat all sides.
    - Cover with a cloth or plastic wrap and let it rise in a warm, draft-free area for 1-1.5 hours, or until doubled in size.
5. **Shape the Loaf:**
    - Punch down the dough to release air bubbles.

- Shape the dough into a loaf or divide into smaller portions for rolls.
- Place in a greased loaf pan or on a parchment-lined baking sheet.

6. **Second Rise:**
   - Cover and let the dough rise for another 30-45 minutes, or until puffy.
7. **Bake:**
   - Preheat your oven to 375°F (190°C).
   - Bake the bread for 30-35 minutes, or until golden brown and the bread sounds hollow when tapped.
8. **Glaze (Optional):**
   - While the bread is baking, you can prepare the glaze. In a small bowl, mix powdered sugar with enough milk or water to make a smooth, drizzle-able glaze.
   - Brush or drizzle the glaze over the warm bread after it comes out of the oven.
9. **Cool:**
   - Allow the bread to cool on a wire rack before slicing.

This Christmas bread is perfect for holiday gatherings, and its sweet, spiced aroma will fill your kitchen with festive cheer. Enjoy!

Chleb Z Białym Serem

Ingredients:

- **For the Dough:**
    - 3 1/2 cups all-purpose flour
    - 1 1/2 cups warm water (110°F or 45°C)
    - 2 tablespoons active dry yeast
    - 1 teaspoon sugar
    - 1 teaspoon salt
    - 1/4 cup olive oil or melted butter
- **For the Cheese Filling:**
    - 1 cup crumbled white cheese (such as feta or ricotta)
    - 1/2 cup chopped fresh herbs (such as parsley, chives, or dill)
    - Optional: 1/4 cup finely chopped onions or garlic

Instructions:

1. **Activate the Yeast:**
    - In a small bowl, combine warm water and sugar. Stir to dissolve.
    - Sprinkle the yeast over the mixture and let it sit for 5-10 minutes, until frothy.
2. **Mix the Dough:**
    - In a large mixing bowl, combine the flour and salt.
    - Make a well in the center and add the activated yeast mixture and olive oil (or melted butter).
    - Mix until a dough forms.
3. **Knead the Dough:**
    - Turn the dough onto a floured surface and knead for about 8-10 minutes, until smooth and elastic.
4. **Prepare the Cheese Filling:**
    - In a bowl, combine the crumbled cheese, chopped herbs, and optional onions or garlic.
5. **First Rise:**
    - Place the dough in a lightly oiled bowl, turning to coat all sides.
    - Cover with a cloth or plastic wrap and let it rise in a warm, draft-free area for 1-1.5 hours, or until doubled in size.
6. **Incorporate the Cheese:**
    - Punch down the dough and turn it out onto a floured surface.
    - Roll out the dough into a rectangle (about 12x16 inches).
    - Spread the cheese mixture evenly over the dough.
    - Roll up the dough tightly from one end to the other to form a log.
7. **Shape the Loaf:**

- Place the rolled dough seam-side down on a greased baking sheet or in a greased loaf pan.
8. **Second Rise:**
    - Cover and let the dough rise for another 30-45 minutes, or until puffy.
9. **Bake:**
    - Preheat your oven to 375°F (190°C).
    - Bake the bread for 30-35 minutes, or until golden brown and the bread sounds hollow when tapped.
10. **Cool:**
    - Allow the bread to cool on a wire rack before slicing.

This cheese-filled bread is savory and satisfying, with a rich, creamy texture from the cheese. Enjoy it warm or at room temperature!

Chleb Bezglutenowy

Ingredients:

- **For the Dough:**
    - 2 cups gluten-free all-purpose flour blend (ensure it includes xanthan gum or guar gum)
    - 1 cup warm water (110°F or 45°C)
    - 1/4 cup olive oil or melted butter
    - 2 tablespoons honey or sugar
    - 2 tablespoons active dry yeast
    - 1 teaspoon salt
    - 1 teaspoon apple cider vinegar
    - Optional: 1/2 cup gluten-free oats or seeds (e.g., sunflower, chia)

Instructions:

1. **Activate the Yeast:**
    - In a small bowl, combine warm water and honey (or sugar). Stir to dissolve.
    - Sprinkle the yeast over the mixture and let it sit for 5-10 minutes, until frothy.
2. **Mix the Dough:**
    - In a large mixing bowl, combine the gluten-free flour blend and salt.
    - Make a well in the center and add the activated yeast mixture, olive oil, and apple cider vinegar.
    - Mix until a thick dough forms. If using, fold in the oats or seeds.
3. **First Rise:**
    - Transfer the dough to a greased loaf pan, smoothing the top with a spatula.
    - Cover with a cloth or plastic wrap and let it rise in a warm, draft-free area for 30-45 minutes, or until slightly puffy.
4. **Bake:**
    - Preheat your oven to 375°F (190°C).
    - Bake the bread for 35-40 minutes, or until golden brown and the bread sounds hollow when tapped.
5. **Cool:**
    - Allow the bread to cool in the pan for 10 minutes, then transfer to a wire rack to cool completely before slicing.

This gluten-free bread is a great base for sandwiches or toasts, offering a soft texture and mild flavor. Enjoy!

Chleb Maślankowy

Ingredients:

- 3 1/2 cups all-purpose flour
- 1 1/2 cups buttermilk (room temperature)
- 1/4 cup sugar
- 1/4 cup melted butter
- 2 tablespoons active dry yeast
- 1 teaspoon salt
- Optional: 1 egg, beaten (for egg wash)

Instructions:

1. **Activate the Yeast:**
     - In a small bowl, combine 1/2 cup of the buttermilk with the sugar. Stir to dissolve.
     - Sprinkle the yeast over the mixture and let it sit for 5-10 minutes, until frothy.
2. **Mix the Dough:**
     - In a large mixing bowl, combine the flour and salt.
     - Make a well in the center and add the activated yeast mixture, the remaining buttermilk, and melted butter.
     - Mix until a dough forms. The dough should be slightly sticky but manageable.
3. **Knead the Dough:**
     - Turn the dough onto a floured surface and knead for about 8-10 minutes, until smooth and elastic.
4. **First Rise:**
     - Place the dough in a lightly oiled bowl, turning to coat all sides.
     - Cover with a cloth or plastic wrap and let it rise in a warm, draft-free area for 1-1.5 hours, or until doubled in size.
5. **Shape the Loaf:**
     - Punch down the dough to release air bubbles.
     - Shape the dough into a loaf and place it in a greased loaf pan.
     - If desired, brush the top with a beaten egg for a golden crust.
6. **Second Rise:**
     - Cover and let the dough rise for another 30-45 minutes, or until puffy.
7. **Bake:**
     - Preheat your oven to 375°F (190°C).
     - Bake the bread for 30-35 minutes, or until golden brown and the bread sounds hollow when tapped.
8. **Cool:**
     - Allow the bread to cool on a wire rack before slicing.

This buttermilk bread is wonderfully soft and has a subtle tang that makes it a tasty addition to any meal. Enjoy!

Chleb Z Marcepanem

Ingredients:

- **For the Dough:**
    - 3 1/2 cups all-purpose flour
    - 1 cup warm milk (110°F or 45°C)
    - 1/2 cup sugar
    - 1/2 cup unsalted butter, softened
    - 2 large eggs
    - 2 tablespoons active dry yeast
    - 1 teaspoon salt
    - 1 teaspoon vanilla extract
    - 1/2 teaspoon almond extract
- **For the Marzipan Filling:**
    - 1/2 cup marzipan, crumbled or cut into small pieces
    - 1/4 cup chopped almonds (optional)
- **For the Glaze (optional):**
    - 1/4 cup powdered sugar
    - 1-2 tablespoons milk or water

Instructions:

1. **Activate the Yeast:**
    - In a small bowl, combine warm milk and sugar. Stir to dissolve.
    - Sprinkle the yeast over the mixture and let it sit for 5-10 minutes, until frothy.
2. **Mix the Dough:**
    - In a large mixing bowl, combine the flour and salt.
    - Make a well in the center and add the activated yeast mixture, softened butter, eggs, vanilla extract, and almond extract.
    - Mix until a dough forms. The dough will be slightly sticky.
3. **Knead the Dough:**
    - Turn the dough onto a floured surface and knead for about 8-10 minutes, until smooth and elastic.
4. **First Rise:**
    - Place the dough in a lightly oiled bowl, turning to coat all sides.
    - Cover with a cloth or plastic wrap and let it rise in a warm, draft-free area for 1-1.5 hours, or until doubled in size.
5. **Incorporate the Marzipan:**
    - Punch down the dough and turn it out onto a floured surface.
    - Roll out the dough into a rectangle (about 12x16 inches).

- Evenly sprinkle the crumbled marzipan and chopped almonds (if using) over the dough.
- Roll up the dough tightly from one end to the other to form a log.

6. **Shape the Loaf:**
   - Place the rolled dough seam-side down on a greased baking sheet or in a greased loaf pan.
7. **Second Rise:**
   - Cover and let the dough rise for another 30-45 minutes, or until puffy.
8. **Bake:**
   - Preheat your oven to 375°F (190°C).
   - Bake the bread for 30-35 minutes, or until golden brown and the bread sounds hollow when tapped.
9. **Glaze (Optional):**
   - While the bread is baking, you can prepare the glaze. In a small bowl, mix powdered sugar with enough milk or water to make a smooth, drizzle-able glaze.
   - Brush or drizzle the glaze over the warm bread after it comes out of the oven.
10. **Cool:**
    - Allow the bread to cool on a wire rack before slicing.

This marzipan bread is slightly sweet with a delightful almond flavor, making it a delicious and special treat. Enjoy it fresh or toasted with a bit of butter!

Chleb Z Cebulą

Ingredients:

- **For the Dough:**
    - 3 1/2 cups all-purpose flour
    - 1 1/2 cups warm water (110°F or 45°C)
    - 2 tablespoons active dry yeast
    - 1 teaspoon sugar
    - 1 teaspoon salt
    - 1/4 cup olive oil
- **For the Onion Filling:**
    - 2 large onions, finely chopped
    - 2 tablespoons olive oil
    - 1 teaspoon sugar (to caramelize onions)
    - Optional: 1 tablespoon chopped fresh thyme or rosemary

Instructions:

1. **Prepare the Onions:**
    - Heat 2 tablespoons of olive oil in a skillet over medium heat.
    - Add the chopped onions and sugar. Cook, stirring frequently, until the onions are soft and caramelized, about 15-20 minutes. Let cool.
2. **Activate the Yeast:**
    - In a small bowl, combine warm water and sugar. Stir to dissolve.
    - Sprinkle the yeast over the mixture and let it sit for 5-10 minutes, until frothy.
3. **Mix the Dough:**
    - In a large mixing bowl, combine the flour and salt.
    - Make a well in the center and add the activated yeast mixture and olive oil.
    - Mix until a dough forms. Fold in the cooled caramelized onions and herbs, if using.
4. **Knead the Dough:**
    - Turn the dough onto a floured surface and knead for about 8-10 minutes, until smooth and elastic.
5. **First Rise:**
    - Place the dough in a lightly oiled bowl, turning to coat all sides.
    - Cover with a cloth or plastic wrap and let it rise in a warm, draft-free area for 1-1.5 hours, or until doubled in size.
6. **Shape the Loaf:**
    - Punch down the dough to release air bubbles.
    - Shape the dough into a loaf and place it in a greased loaf pan or on a parchment-lined baking sheet.

7. **Second Rise:**
     - Cover and let the dough rise for another 30-45 minutes, or until puffy.
8. **Bake:**
     - Preheat your oven to 375°F (190°C).
     - Bake the bread for 30-35 minutes, or until golden brown and the bread sounds hollow when tapped.
9. **Cool:**
     - Allow the bread to cool on a wire rack before slicing.

This onion bread offers a savory twist with the sweet and rich flavor of caramelized onions throughout. Enjoy it fresh or toasted!

Chleb Żytni Na Zakwasie

Ingredients:

- **For the Sourdough Starter:**
    - 1/2 cup rye flour
    - 1/2 cup water
    - 1 tablespoon active rye sourdough starter (or a pinch of yeast if starting from scratch)
- **For the Dough:**
    - 2 cups rye flour
    - 1 cup all-purpose flour
    - 1 1/2 cups water
    - 1 teaspoon salt
    - 1 tablespoon honey or sugar
    - 1/2 cup sourdough starter (from above)

Instructions:

1. **Prepare the Sourdough Starter:**
    - Mix the rye flour and water in a bowl. Add the sourdough starter or a pinch of yeast if starting from scratch.
    - Cover loosely and let it sit at room temperature for 12-24 hours until bubbly and active.
2. **Mix the Dough:**
    - In a large bowl, combine the rye flour and all-purpose flour.
    - Add the sourdough starter, water, salt, and honey. Mix until well combined. The dough will be sticky and dense.
3. **Knead the Dough:**
    - Turn the dough onto a floured surface and knead gently for about 5 minutes. It may remain somewhat sticky.
4. **First Rise:**
    - Transfer the dough to a lightly oiled bowl, turning to coat all sides.
    - Cover with a cloth or plastic wrap and let it rise in a warm, draft-free area for 1-2 hours, or until doubled in size.
5. **Shape the Loaf:**
    - Punch down the dough and turn it out onto a floured surface.
    - Shape into a loaf and place it in a greased or lined loaf pan, or shape into a round and place on a parchment-lined baking sheet.
6. **Second Rise:**
    - Cover and let the dough rise for another 30-45 minutes, or until puffy.
7. **Bake:**

        - Preheat your oven to 450°F (230°C).
        - Bake the bread for 30-35 minutes, or until the crust is dark brown and the bread sounds hollow when tapped.
8. **Cool:**
        - Allow the bread to cool on a wire rack before slicing.

This rye sourdough bread has a hearty flavor with a tangy twist from the sourdough starter, making it a great choice for sandwiches or hearty meals. Enjoy!

Chleb Z Siemieniem Lniany

Ingredients:

- **For the Dough:**
    - 3 1/2 cups all-purpose flour
    - 1 cup warm water (110°F or 45°C)
    - 2 tablespoons active dry yeast
    - 1/4 cup honey or sugar
    - 1/4 cup olive oil or melted butter
    - 1 teaspoon salt
    - 1/2 cup ground flaxseeds
    - 1/4 cup whole flaxseeds (optional, for topping)

Instructions:

1. **Activate the Yeast:**
    - In a small bowl, combine warm water and honey (or sugar). Stir to dissolve.
    - Sprinkle the yeast over the mixture and let it sit for 5-10 minutes, until frothy.
2. **Mix the Dough:**
    - In a large mixing bowl, combine the flour, salt, and ground flaxseeds.
    - Make a well in the center and add the activated yeast mixture and olive oil (or melted butter).
    - Mix until a dough forms. It will be slightly sticky.
3. **Knead the Dough:**
    - Turn the dough onto a floured surface and knead for about 8-10 minutes, until smooth and elastic.
4. **First Rise:**
    - Place the dough in a lightly oiled bowl, turning to coat all sides.
    - Cover with a cloth or plastic wrap and let it rise in a warm, draft-free area for 1-1.5 hours, or until doubled in size.
5. **Shape the Loaf:**
    - Punch down the dough and turn it out onto a floured surface.
    - Shape into a loaf and place it in a greased loaf pan.
    - If using, sprinkle whole flaxseeds on top of the dough and gently press them in.
6. **Second Rise:**
    - Cover and let the dough rise for another 30-45 minutes, or until puffy.
7. **Bake:**
    - Preheat your oven to 375°F (190°C).
    - Bake the bread for 30-35 minutes, or until golden brown and the bread sounds hollow when tapped.
8. **Cool:**
    - Allow the bread to cool on a wire rack before slicing.

This flaxseed bread is wholesome and slightly nutty, with the added benefit of flaxseeds, which are rich in omega-3 fatty acids. Enjoy it fresh or toasted!

Chleb Tarty

Ingredients:

- **For the Dough:**
    - 3 1/2 cups all-purpose flour
    - 1 1/2 cups warm water (110°F or 45°C)
    - 2 tablespoons active dry yeast
    - 1 teaspoon sugar
    - 1 teaspoon salt
    - 1/4 cup olive oil or melted butter
- **For the Grated Ingredients:**
    - 1 cup grated cheese (such as cheddar, Parmesan, or a mix)
    - Optional: 1/2 cup grated vegetables (such as zucchini or carrots)
    - Optional: 1/4 cup finely chopped fresh herbs (such as rosemary or thyme)

Instructions:

1. **Activate the Yeast:**
    - In a small bowl, combine warm water and sugar. Stir to dissolve.
    - Sprinkle the yeast over the mixture and let it sit for 5-10 minutes, until frothy.
2. **Mix the Dough:**
    - In a large mixing bowl, combine the flour and salt.
    - Make a well in the center and add the activated yeast mixture and olive oil (or melted butter).
    - Mix until a dough forms.
3. **Incorporate the Grated Ingredients:**
    - Gently fold in the grated cheese, and if using, the grated vegetables and chopped herbs.
4. **Knead the Dough:**
    - Turn the dough onto a floured surface and knead for about 8-10 minutes, until smooth and elastic.
5. **First Rise:**
    - Place the dough in a lightly oiled bowl, turning to coat all sides.
    - Cover with a cloth or plastic wrap and let it rise in a warm, draft-free area for 1-1.5 hours, or until doubled in size.
6. **Shape the Loaf:**
    - Punch down the dough and turn it out onto a floured surface.
    - Shape into a loaf and place it in a greased loaf pan, or shape it into a round loaf and place it on a parchment-lined baking sheet.
7. **Second Rise:**
    - Cover and let the dough rise for another 30-45 minutes, or until puffy.

8. **Bake:**
    - Preheat your oven to 375°F (190°C).
    - Bake the bread for 30-35 minutes, or until golden brown and the bread sounds hollow when tapped.
9. **Cool:**
    - Allow the bread to cool on a wire rack before slicing.

This grated bread is flavorful and versatile, with a rich taste from the cheese and optional vegetables. Enjoy it fresh, toasted, or as an accompaniment to soups and salads!

Chleb Miodowy

Ingredients:

- **For the Dough:**
    - 3 1/2 cups all-purpose flour
    - 1 cup warm milk (110°F or 45°C)
    - 1/4 cup honey
    - 1/4 cup melted butter or vegetable oil
    - 2 tablespoons active dry yeast
    - 1 teaspoon salt
    - 1 large egg

Instructions:

1. **Activate the Yeast:**
    - In a small bowl, combine warm milk and honey. Stir to dissolve.
    - Sprinkle the yeast over the mixture and let it sit for 5-10 minutes, until frothy.
2. **Mix the Dough:**
    - In a large mixing bowl, combine the flour and salt.
    - Make a well in the center and add the activated yeast mixture, melted butter (or oil), and egg.
    - Mix until a dough forms.
3. **Knead the Dough:**
    - Turn the dough onto a floured surface and knead for about 8-10 minutes, until smooth and elastic.
4. **First Rise:**
    - Place the dough in a lightly oiled bowl, turning to coat all sides.
    - Cover with a cloth or plastic wrap and let it rise in a warm, draft-free area for 1-1.5 hours, or until doubled in size.
5. **Shape the Loaf:**
    - Punch down the dough and turn it out onto a floured surface.
    - Shape into a loaf and place it in a greased loaf pan.
6. **Second Rise:**
    - Cover and let the dough rise for another 30-45 minutes, or until puffy.
7. **Bake:**
    - Preheat your oven to 375°F (190°C).
    - Bake the bread for 30-35 minutes, or until golden brown and the bread sounds hollow when tapped.
8. **Cool:**
    - Allow the bread to cool on a wire rack before slicing.

This honey bread has a slight sweetness and a soft, tender crumb. Enjoy it fresh or toasted with a bit of butter!

Chleb Góralski Żytni

Ingredients:

- **For the Dough:**
    - 2 cups rye flour
    - 1 cup all-purpose flour
    - 1 1/2 cups warm water (110°F or 45°C)
    - 2 tablespoons active dry yeast
    - 1 tablespoon honey or sugar
    - 1 teaspoon salt
    - 1 tablespoon caraway seeds (optional)

Instructions:

1. **Activate the Yeast:**
    - In a small bowl, combine warm water and honey (or sugar). Stir to dissolve.
    - Sprinkle the yeast over the mixture and let it sit for 5-10 minutes, until frothy.
2. **Mix the Dough:**
    - In a large mixing bowl, combine the rye flour, all-purpose flour, salt, and caraway seeds (if using).
    - Make a well in the center and add the activated yeast mixture.
    - Mix until a thick, sticky dough forms.
3. **Knead the Dough:**
    - Turn the dough onto a floured surface and knead gently for about 5-7 minutes. Rye dough will be stickier and less elastic than wheat dough.
4. **First Rise:**
    - Place the dough in a lightly oiled bowl, turning to coat all sides.
    - Cover with a cloth or plastic wrap and let it rise in a warm, draft-free area for 1-1.5 hours, or until doubled in size.
5. **Shape the Loaf:**
    - Punch down the dough and turn it out onto a floured surface.
    - Shape into a loaf and place it in a greased loaf pan or on a parchment-lined baking sheet.
6. **Second Rise:**
    - Cover and let the dough rise for another 30-45 minutes, or until puffy.
7. **Bake:**
    - Preheat your oven to 375°F (190°C).
    - Bake the bread for 35-40 minutes, or until dark brown and the bread sounds hollow when tapped.
8. **Cool:**
    - Allow the bread to cool on a wire rack before slicing.

This rye bread has a rustic, dense texture and a robust flavor, ideal for hearty sandwiches or served with traditional Polish dishes. Enjoy!

Chleb Na Wodzie

Ingredients:

- **For the Dough:**
    - 4 cups all-purpose flour
    - 1 1/2 cups warm water (110°F or 45°C)
    - 2 tablespoons active dry yeast
    - 1 tablespoon sugar
    - 1 teaspoon salt
    - 2 tablespoons olive oil (optional)

Instructions:

1. **Activate the Yeast:**
    - In a small bowl, combine warm water and sugar. Stir to dissolve.
    - Sprinkle the yeast over the mixture and let it sit for 5-10 minutes, until frothy.
2. **Mix the Dough:**
    - In a large mixing bowl, combine the flour and salt.
    - Make a well in the center and add the activated yeast mixture and olive oil (if using).
    - Mix until a dough forms.
3. **Knead the Dough:**
    - Turn the dough onto a floured surface and knead for about 8-10 minutes, until smooth and elastic.
4. **First Rise:**
    - Place the dough in a lightly oiled bowl, turning to coat all sides.
    - Cover with a cloth or plastic wrap and let it rise in a warm, draft-free area for 1-1.5 hours, or until doubled in size.
5. **Shape the Loaf:**
    - Punch down the dough and turn it out onto a floured surface.
    - Shape into a loaf and place it in a greased loaf pan or on a parchment-lined baking sheet.
6. **Second Rise:**
    - Cover and let the dough rise for another 30-45 minutes, or until puffy.
7. **Bake:**
    - Preheat your oven to 375°F (190°C).
    - Bake the bread for 30-35 minutes, or until golden brown and the bread sounds hollow when tapped.
8. **Cool:**
    - Allow the bread to cool on a wire rack before slicing.

This water bread is simple yet satisfying, with a light and airy texture perfect for everyday use. Enjoy it fresh or toasted!

Chleb Z Orzechami

Ingredients:

- **For the Dough:**
    - 3 1/2 cups all-purpose flour
    - 1 1/2 cups warm water (110°F or 45°C)
    - 2 tablespoons active dry yeast
    - 1 tablespoon honey or sugar
    - 1 teaspoon salt
    - 1/4 cup olive oil or melted butter
- **For the Nuts:**
    - 1 cup mixed nuts (such as walnuts, pecans, or almonds), chopped

Instructions:

1. **Activate the Yeast:**
    - In a small bowl, combine warm water and honey (or sugar). Stir to dissolve.
    - Sprinkle the yeast over the mixture and let it sit for 5-10 minutes, until frothy.
2. **Mix the Dough:**
    - In a large mixing bowl, combine the flour and salt.
    - Make a well in the center and add the activated yeast mixture and olive oil (or melted butter).
    - Mix until a dough forms. Gently fold in the chopped nuts.
3. **Knead the Dough:**
    - Turn the dough onto a floured surface and knead for about 8-10 minutes, until smooth and elastic.
4. **First Rise:**
    - Place the dough in a lightly oiled bowl, turning to coat all sides.
    - Cover with a cloth or plastic wrap and let it rise in a warm, draft-free area for 1-1.5 hours, or until doubled in size.
5. **Shape the Loaf:**
    - Punch down the dough and turn it out onto a floured surface.
    - Shape into a loaf and place it in a greased loaf pan or on a parchment-lined baking sheet.
6. **Second Rise:**
    - Cover and let the dough rise for another 30-45 minutes, or until puffy.
7. **Bake:**
    - Preheat your oven to 375°F (190°C).
    - Bake the bread for 30-35 minutes, or until golden brown and the bread sounds hollow when tapped.
8. **Cool:**

- Allow the bread to cool on a wire rack before slicing.

This nut bread has a delightful crunch and a nutty flavor that pairs well with both sweet and savory toppings. Enjoy it fresh or toasted!

Chleb Na Mące Przemysłowej

Ingredients:

- **For the Dough:**
    - 3 1/2 cups all-purpose or bread flour
    - 1 1/2 cups warm water (110°F or 45°C)
    - 2 tablespoons active dry yeast
    - 1 tablespoon sugar
    - 1 teaspoon salt
    - 2 tablespoons olive oil or melted butter

Instructions:

1. **Activate the Yeast:**
    - In a small bowl, combine warm water and sugar. Stir to dissolve.
    - Sprinkle the yeast over the mixture and let it sit for 5-10 minutes, until frothy.
2. **Mix the Dough:**
    - In a large mixing bowl, combine the flour and salt.
    - Make a well in the center and add the activated yeast mixture and olive oil (or melted butter).
    - Mix until a dough forms.
3. **Knead the Dough:**
    - Turn the dough onto a floured surface and knead for about 8-10 minutes, until smooth and elastic.
4. **First Rise:**
    - Place the dough in a lightly oiled bowl, turning to coat all sides.
    - Cover with a cloth or plastic wrap and let it rise in a warm, draft-free area for 1-1.5 hours, or until doubled in size.
5. **Shape the Loaf:**
    - Punch down the dough and turn it out onto a floured surface.
    - Shape into a loaf and place it in a greased loaf pan or on a parchment-lined baking sheet.
6. **Second Rise:**
    - Cover and let the dough rise for another 30-45 minutes, or until puffy.
7. **Bake:**
    - Preheat your oven to 375°F (190°C).
    - Bake the bread for 30-35 minutes, or until golden brown and the bread sounds hollow when tapped.
8. **Cool:**
    - Allow the bread to cool on a wire rack before slicing.

This basic bread recipe is perfect for everyday use and can be customized with additional ingredients like herbs, seeds, or cheese if desired.

Chleb Na Zakwasie Żytnim

Ingredients:

- **For the Sourdough Starter:**
    - 1/2 cup rye flour
    - 1/2 cup water
    - 1 tablespoon sourdough starter (from a previous batch or store-bought)
- **For the Dough:**
    - 2 cups rye flour
    - 1 cup all-purpose flour
    - 1 1/2 cups warm water (110°F or 45°C)
    - 1 teaspoon salt
    - 1 tablespoon honey (optional, for a touch of sweetness)

Instructions:

1. **Prepare the Sourdough Starter:**
    - In a small bowl, combine 1/2 cup rye flour and 1/2 cup water. Add the sourdough starter.
    - Stir well and cover loosely. Let it sit at room temperature for 12-24 hours until bubbly and active.
2. **Mix the Dough:**
    - In a large mixing bowl, combine the rye flour and all-purpose flour.
    - Make a well in the center and add 1 1/2 cups of warm water, the prepared sourdough starter, and salt. If using, add the honey.
    - Mix until a sticky dough forms.
3. **Knead the Dough:**
    - Turn the dough onto a lightly floured surface and knead gently for about 5-7 minutes. Rye dough will be sticky and less elastic than wheat dough.
4. **First Rise:**
    - Place the dough in a lightly oiled bowl, turning to coat all sides.
    - Cover with a cloth or plastic wrap and let it rise in a warm, draft-free area for 1-2 hours, or until doubled in size.
5. **Shape the Loaf:**
    - Punch down the dough and turn it out onto a floured surface.
    - Shape into a loaf and place it in a greased loaf pan or on a parchment-lined baking sheet.
6. **Second Rise:**
    - Cover and let the dough rise for another 30-45 minutes, or until puffy.
7. **Bake:**
    - Preheat your oven to 375°F (190°C).
    - Bake the bread for 35-40 minutes, or until the crust is dark brown and the bread sounds hollow when tapped.
8. **Cool:**
    - Allow the bread to cool on a wire rack before slicing.

Tips:

- **Starter Care:** If you're using a store-bought starter or a starter from a previous batch, make sure it's active and bubbly. If it's not, feed it with equal parts flour and water for 24 hours before using it.
- **Texture:** Rye dough is denser and stickier than wheat dough. It's normal for it not to rise as much as wheat-based bread.
- **Flavor:** Rye bread has a strong, earthy flavor that improves with time. It's often best enjoyed a day or two after baking.

Enjoy your traditional rye sourdough bread with its rich, hearty flavor and satisfying texture!

Chleb Z Kiełbasą

Ingredients:

- **For the Dough:**
    - 3 1/2 cups all-purpose flour
    - 1 1/2 cups warm water (110°F or 45°C)
    - 2 tablespoons active dry yeast
    - 1 tablespoon sugar
    - 1 teaspoon salt
    - 2 tablespoons olive oil or melted butter
- **For the Filling:**
    - 1 cup cooked sausage, diced (e.g., kielbasa or any preferred type)
    - Optional: 1/2 cup shredded cheese (e.g., cheddar or gouda)

Instructions:

1. **Activate the Yeast:**
    - In a small bowl, combine warm water and sugar. Stir to dissolve.
    - Sprinkle the yeast over the mixture and let it sit for 5-10 minutes, until frothy.
2. **Mix the Dough:**
    - In a large mixing bowl, combine the flour and salt.
    - Make a well in the center and add the activated yeast mixture and olive oil (or melted butter).
    - Mix until a dough forms.
3. **Incorporate the Sausage:**
    - Gently fold in the diced sausage and optional shredded cheese.
4. **Knead the Dough:**
    - Turn the dough onto a floured surface and knead for about 8-10 minutes, until smooth and elastic.
5. **First Rise:**
    - Place the dough in a lightly oiled bowl, turning to coat all sides.
    - Cover with a cloth or plastic wrap and let it rise in a warm, draft-free area for 1-1.5 hours, or until doubled in size.
6. **Shape the Loaf:**
    - Punch down the dough and turn it out onto a floured surface.
    - Shape into a loaf and place it in a greased loaf pan or on a parchment-lined baking sheet.
7. **Second Rise:**
    - Cover and let the dough rise for another 30-45 minutes, or until puffy.
8. **Bake:**
    - Preheat your oven to 375°F (190°C).

- Bake the bread for 30-35 minutes, or until golden brown and the bread sounds hollow when tapped.
9. **Cool:**
    - Allow the bread to cool on a wire rack before slicing.

This savory bread combines the rich flavors of sausage with a soft, fresh loaf, making it perfect for sandwiches or served with a hearty soup. Enjoy!

Chleb Na Owsianych Płatkach

Ingredients:

- **For the Dough:**
    - 3 cups all-purpose flour
    - 1 cup oat flakes (rolled oats)
    - 1 1/2 cups warm water (110°F or 45°C)
    - 2 tablespoons active dry yeast
    - 1 tablespoon honey or sugar
    - 1 teaspoon salt
    - 1/4 cup olive oil or melted butter

Instructions:

1. **Activate the Yeast:**
    - In a small bowl, combine warm water and honey (or sugar). Stir to dissolve.
    - Sprinkle the yeast over the mixture and let it sit for 5-10 minutes, until frothy.
2. **Mix the Dough:**
    - In a large mixing bowl, combine the flour, oat flakes, and salt.
    - Make a well in the center and add the activated yeast mixture and olive oil (or melted butter).
    - Mix until a dough forms.
3. **Knead the Dough:**
    - Turn the dough onto a floured surface and knead for about 8-10 minutes, until smooth and elastic.
4. **First Rise:**
    - Place the dough in a lightly oiled bowl, turning to coat all sides.
    - Cover with a cloth or plastic wrap and let it rise in a warm, draft-free area for 1-1.5 hours, or until doubled in size.
5. **Shape the Loaf:**
    - Punch down the dough and turn it out onto a floured surface.
    - Shape into a loaf and place it in a greased loaf pan or on a parchment-lined baking sheet.
6. **Second Rise:**
    - Cover and let the dough rise for another 30-45 minutes, or until puffy.
7. **Bake:**
    - Preheat your oven to 375°F (190°C).
    - Bake the bread for 30-35 minutes, or until golden brown and the bread sounds hollow when tapped.
8. **Cool:**
    - Allow the bread to cool on a wire rack before slicing.

The oat flakes give this bread a hearty, nutty flavor and a pleasing texture. Enjoy it fresh or toasted!

Chleb Z Rodzynkami

Ingredients:

- **For the Dough:**
    - 3 1/2 cups all-purpose flour
    - 1 1/2 cups warm milk (110°F or 45°C)
    - 2 tablespoons active dry yeast
    - 1/4 cup sugar
    - 1 teaspoon salt
    - 1/4 cup unsalted butter, melted
    - 1 large egg
- **For the Raisins:**
    - 1 cup raisins
    - Optional: 1 teaspoon ground cinnamon (for added flavor)

Instructions:

1. **Prepare the Raisins:**
    - If you like, you can soak the raisins in warm water for 10 minutes to plump them up. Drain well before using.
2. **Activate the Yeast:**
    - In a small bowl, combine warm milk and sugar. Stir to dissolve.
    - Sprinkle the yeast over the mixture and let it sit for 5-10 minutes, until frothy.
3. **Mix the Dough:**
    - In a large mixing bowl, combine the flour and salt.
    - Make a well in the center and add the activated yeast mixture, melted butter, and egg.
    - Mix until a dough forms.
4. **Incorporate the Raisins:**
    - Gently fold in the raisins (and cinnamon if using) until evenly distributed.
5. **Knead the Dough:**
    - Turn the dough onto a floured surface and knead for about 8-10 minutes, until smooth and elastic.
6. **First Rise:**
    - Place the dough in a lightly oiled bowl, turning to coat all sides.
    - Cover with a cloth or plastic wrap and let it rise in a warm, draft-free area for 1-1.5 hours, or until doubled in size.
7. **Shape the Loaf:**
    - Punch down the dough and turn it out onto a floured surface.
    - Shape into a loaf and place it in a greased loaf pan or on a parchment-lined baking sheet.

8. **Second Rise:**
    - Cover and let the dough rise for another 30-45 minutes, or until puffy.
9. **Bake:**
    - Preheat your oven to 375°F (190°C).
    - Bake the bread for 30-35 minutes, or until golden brown and the bread sounds hollow when tapped.
10. **Cool:**
    - Allow the bread to cool on a wire rack before slicing.

This raisin bread is soft, slightly sweet, and perfect for toasting. Enjoy it fresh with a bit of butter or your favorite spread!

Chleb Z Chrzanem

Ingredients:

- **For the Dough:**
    - 3 1/2 cups all-purpose flour
    - 1 1/2 cups warm water (110°F or 45°C)
    - 2 tablespoons active dry yeast
    - 1 tablespoon sugar
    - 1 teaspoon salt
    - 1/4 cup olive oil or melted butter
    - 2-3 tablespoons prepared horseradish (adjust to taste)

Instructions:

1. **Activate the Yeast:**
    - In a small bowl, combine warm water and sugar. Stir to dissolve.
    - Sprinkle the yeast over the mixture and let it sit for 5-10 minutes, until frothy.
2. **Mix the Dough:**
    - In a large mixing bowl, combine the flour and salt.
    - Make a well in the center and add the activated yeast mixture, olive oil (or melted butter), and prepared horseradish.
    - Mix until a dough forms.
3. **Knead the Dough:**
    - Turn the dough onto a floured surface and knead for about 8-10 minutes, until smooth and elastic.
4. **First Rise:**
    - Place the dough in a lightly oiled bowl, turning to coat all sides.
    - Cover with a cloth or plastic wrap and let it rise in a warm, draft-free area for 1-1.5 hours, or until doubled in size.
5. **Shape the Loaf:**
    - Punch down the dough and turn it out onto a floured surface.
    - Shape into a loaf and place it in a greased loaf pan or on a parchment-lined baking sheet.
6. **Second Rise:**
    - Cover and let the dough rise for another 30-45 minutes, or until puffy.
7. **Bake:**
    - Preheat your oven to 375°F (190°C).
    - Bake the bread for 30-35 minutes, or until golden brown and the bread sounds hollow when tapped.
8. **Cool:**
    - Allow the bread to cool on a wire rack before slicing.

Tips:

- **Horseradish:** Adjust the amount of horseradish to your taste. Fresh horseradish can be used if available, but prepared horseradish from a jar works well for this recipe.
- **Texture:** This bread will have a subtle horseradish flavor, which can be enhanced with more or less horseradish depending on your preference.

Enjoy your Chleb Z Chrzanem fresh or toasted, perfect with meats or as a unique sandwich bread!

Chleb Wiejski Z Ziołami

Ingredients:

- **For the Dough:**
    - 3 1/2 cups all-purpose flour
    - 1 1/2 cups warm water (110°F or 45°C)
    - 2 tablespoons active dry yeast
    - 1 tablespoon sugar
    - 1 teaspoon salt
    - 2 tablespoons olive oil
    - 1/4 cup fresh herbs (such as rosemary, thyme, oregano, or a mix), chopped or 2 tablespoons dried herbs

Instructions:

1. **Activate the Yeast:**
    - In a small bowl, combine warm water and sugar. Stir to dissolve.
    - Sprinkle the yeast over the mixture and let it sit for 5-10 minutes, until frothy.
2. **Mix the Dough:**
    - In a large mixing bowl, combine the flour and salt.
    - Make a well in the center and add the activated yeast mixture and olive oil.
    - Stir in the chopped or dried herbs.
    - Mix until a dough forms.
3. **Knead the Dough:**
    - Turn the dough onto a floured surface and knead for about 8-10 minutes, until smooth and elastic.
4. **First Rise:**
    - Place the dough in a lightly oiled bowl, turning to coat all sides.
    - Cover with a cloth or plastic wrap and let it rise in a warm, draft-free area for 1-1.5 hours, or until doubled in size.
5. **Shape the Loaf:**
    - Punch down the dough and turn it out onto a floured surface.
    - Shape into a loaf and place it in a greased loaf pan or on a parchment-lined baking sheet. You can also shape it into a round loaf if preferred.
6. **Second Rise:**
    - Cover and let the dough rise for another 30-45 minutes, or until puffy.
7. **Bake:**
    - Preheat your oven to 375°F (190°C).
    - Bake the bread for 30-35 minutes, or until golden brown and the bread sounds hollow when tapped.
8. **Cool:**
    - Allow the bread to cool on a wire rack before slicing.

Tips:

- **Herb Variations:** Feel free to experiment with different combinations of herbs based on your preferences or what you have on hand.
- **Texture:** For a slightly crisper crust, you can place a pan of water in the oven while baking to create steam.

This herb-infused country bread is aromatic and flavorful, making it a wonderful addition to any meal. Enjoy it fresh, or toasted with a bit of butter or olive oil!

Chleb Z Papryką

Ingredients:

- **For the Dough:**
    - 3 1/2 cups all-purpose flour
    - 1 1/2 cups warm water (110°F or 45°C)
    - 2 tablespoons active dry yeast
    - 1 tablespoon sugar
    - 1 teaspoon salt
    - 1/4 cup olive oil
    - 1 cup bell peppers (red, yellow, or green), roasted and finely chopped

Instructions:

1. **Prepare the Peppers:**
    - Roast or sauté the bell peppers until tender. If roasting, place them under the broiler or in a hot oven until charred, then peel and finely chop. If sautéing, cook in a pan with a little oil until softened.
2. **Activate the Yeast:**
    - In a small bowl, combine warm water and sugar. Stir to dissolve.
    - Sprinkle the yeast over the mixture and let it sit for 5-10 minutes, until frothy.
3. **Mix the Dough:**
    - In a large mixing bowl, combine the flour and salt.
    - Make a well in the center and add the activated yeast mixture and olive oil.
    - Stir in the chopped bell peppers.
    - Mix until a dough forms.
4. **Knead the Dough:**
    - Turn the dough onto a floured surface and knead for about 8-10 minutes, until smooth and elastic.
5. **First Rise:**
    - Place the dough in a lightly oiled bowl, turning to coat all sides.
    - Cover with a cloth or plastic wrap and let it rise in a warm, draft-free area for 1-1.5 hours, or until doubled in size.
6. **Shape the Loaf:**
    - Punch down the dough and turn it out onto a floured surface.
    - Shape into a loaf and place it in a greased loaf pan or on a parchment-lined baking sheet.
7. **Second Rise:**
    - Cover and let the dough rise for another 30-45 minutes, or until puffy.
8. **Bake:**
    - Preheat your oven to 375°F (190°C).

- Bake the bread for 30-35 minutes, or until golden brown and the bread sounds hollow when tapped.
9. **Cool:**
    - Allow the bread to cool on a wire rack before slicing.

Tips:

- **Pepper Preparation:** Ensure the peppers are well-drained if you roasted them, as excess moisture can affect the dough's texture.
- **Flavor Enhancements:** You can add herbs like oregano or basil to complement the peppers if desired.

This bread offers a burst of flavor with every slice, making it a great choice for sandwiches or served alongside your favorite dishes. Enjoy!

www.ingramcontent.com/pod-product-compliance
Lightning Source LLC
LaVergne TN
LVHW081604060526
838201LV00054B/2073